MISSISSIPPI

Past and Present

Amy Sterling Casil

rosen publishing's
rosen central®

New York

To the beautiful people of Mississippi, especially the residents of Clarksdale and those near the "crossroads"

Published in 2011 by The Rosen Publishing Group, Inc.
29 East 21st Street, New York, NY 10010

First Edition

Library of Congress Cataloging-in-Publication Data

Casil, Amy Sterling.
Mississippi: past and present / Amy Sterling Casil. — 1st ed.
    p. cm. — (The United States: past and present)
Includes bibliographical references and index.
ISBN 978-1-4358-9485-3 (library binding) —
ISBN 978-1-4358-9512-6 (pbk. book) —
ISBN 978-1-4358-9546-1 (6-pack)
1. Mississippi—Juvenile literature. I. Title.
F341.3.C37 2011
976.2—dc22

2009054262

Manufactured in Malaysia

CPSIA Compliance Information: Batch #S10YA: For further information, contact Rosen Publishing, New York, New York, at 1-800-237-9932.

On the cover: Top left: This picture shows French missionary and explorer Jacques Marquette. Top right: A cotton harvester works a field in Clarksdale, Mississippi. Bottom: The sun rises over the Mississippi River.

Contents

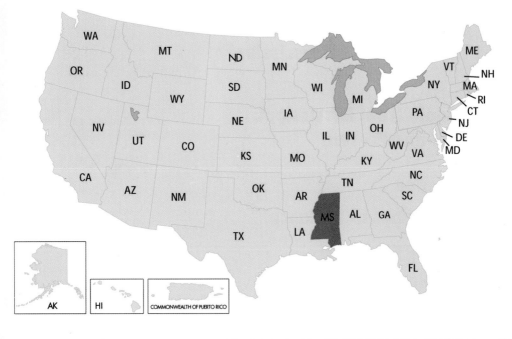

Mississippi became the twentieth state to join the United States in 1817. It was originally part of land that had been disputed between the United States and Spain.

Introduction

Mississippi is the namesake state of the Mississippi River. One of the world's best-known rivers, the Mississippi is the tenth largest river in the world and, together with the Missouri River, part of the longest river system in North America.

A state of contrasts, with a dramatic human history, Mississippi is one of the states that allowed slavery before the Civil War began in 1861. It was the home state of Jefferson Davis, who served as the president of the Confederate States of America during the Civil War period.

Mississippi is also home to courageous civil rights leaders such as Medgar Evers and Fannie Lou Hamer. Primarily because its economy relies on agriculture, which often cannot support many high-paying jobs, Mississippi has for many generations been America's poorest state, with the lowest per-person income. Nevertheless, it is a state rich in history and culture.

Mississippi is one of the least urbanized states in the nation. Only about 47 percent of Mississippians live in areas defined as urban, and the rest live in rural areas. The largest city is Jackson, the capital. Other cities include Biloxi, Greenville, Hattiesburg, Meridian, and Gulfport. Although many communities in Mississippi remain poor today, its per-capita income growth has been among the top five states each year since 2000.

Mississippi experienced conflict and triumph during the civil rights movement in the 1950s and 1960s. Mississippi schools remained segregated long after an important U.S. Supreme Court decision in the 1950s said that states could not provide different schools for students of different races. Mississippi schools, after many years of work on the part of civil rights advocates, became desegregated in 1970.

Some of America's most famous and celebrated authors, musicians, and performers were born in Mississippi, from television host Oprah Winfrey to Elvis Presley, the singer who was called the King of Rock and Roll. Mississippi is also the birthplace of Jim Henson, the creator of the Muppets, and of Nobel Prize–winning author William Faulkner.

Chapter 1

THE GEOGRAPHY OF MISSISSIPPI

Mississippi is located in the southeastern United States. It is bordered on the north by Tennessee, on the east by Alabama, on the south by the Gulf of Mexico and Louisiana, and on the west by Louisiana and Arkansas. The Mississippi River forms nearly all of Mississippi's western boundary.

With an area of 48,434 square miles (125,443 square kilometers), Mississippi is the thirty-second largest state in the United States. The state measures about 330 miles (530 km) from north to south and about 180 miles (290 km) from east to west. The lowest elevation in Mississippi is sea level at the Gulf of Mexico, and the highest elevation is 806 feet (246 meters), at the top of Woodall Mountain in the northeast part of the state. Along the Gulf of Mexico, Mississippi's coastline is 44 miles (71 km) long.

Most of Mississippi is part of the East Gulf Coastal Plain, which extends from southeastern Louisiana over most of Mississippi and includes parts of western Tennessee and Kentucky, the southwestern portion of Alabama, and the Florida panhandle. The northern portion of Mississippi is part of the Mississippi Alluvial Plain, which is also known as the Delta region. The Mississippi Alluvial Plain (Delta) is narrow in the south and widens north of Vicksburg. The region has rich soil, partly made up of silt deposited by floodwaters

7

The Mississippi River Bridge is located in Vicksburg, Mississippi. Shown in the background is the Ameristar riverboat casino.

of the Mississippi River. The East Gulf Coastal Plain is primarily comprised of low hills, such as the Pine Hills in the south and the North Central Hills, which include the Hill Country featured in the novels of author William Faulkner.

The most important river of the state is the Mississippi River. Its tributaries are the Yazoo and Big Black rivers. In central and eastern Mississippi, streams flowing south to the Gulf of Mexico include the Pearl and Pascagoula rivers. Mississippi's largest lakes are created by dams. These larger lakes include Ross Barnett Reservoir on the Pearl River, Arkabutla Lake on the Coldwater River, and Grenada Lake on the Yalobusha River.

Weather

Most of Mississippi's climate is warm and humid. Northern Mississippi in the Delta region averages about 50 inches (127 centimeters) of rainfall a year, while the southern portions of the state on the Gulf of Mexico receive more than 60 inches (152 cm) of rain a year. The highest recorded temperature was 115 degrees Fahrenheit (46 degrees Celsius) recorded at Holly Springs in northern Mississippi in 1930. The lowest recorded tempera-

In August 2005, Hurricane Katrina struck the Gulf Coast of Louisiana and Mississippi.

ture occurred in 1966 in Corinth, where the temperature fell to -18°F (-8°C). Although Louisiana and Texas may be better known for being hit with extreme hurricanes, southern Mississippi in the Gulf area also experiences severe hurricanes. Some of the worst hurricanes affecting Mississippi included Hurricane Katrina in 2005, which also devastated New Orleans, Hurricane Camille in 1965, and Hurricane Elena in 1985.

Plants and Animals

With its warm, rainy, and humid weather, Mississippi is home to many diverse plants and animals. The state's official land mammals

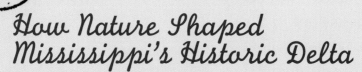

How Nature Shaped Mississippi's Historic Delta

According to the National Park Service, "Much of what is profoundly American— what people love about America—has come from the Delta, which is often called 'the cradle of American culture.'" The Mississippi Delta area began as a deep valley eroded by the Mississippi River during the Pleistocene era, which was the time of the last ice age.

Explorers, including Hernando de Soto in 1543, were the first Europeans to witness the flooding of the Mississippi River. According to historical records, nine large floods were recorded between 1782 and 1850. The most devastating flood in American history occurred in 1927, when the Mississippi River broke through levees in seven states (Arkansas, Illinois, Kentucky, Louisiana, Mississippi, Missouri, and Tennessee). The flood covered an area of approximately 26,000 square miles (67,340 sq km). Although the flood caused devastation, it also deposited rich soil.

Because of the rich soil, the original economy of the Delta area was based on agriculture. Cotton became the most common crop in the early nineteenth century. It was grown on plantations, which were owned by wealthy cotton growers who used slaves to pick the cotton. The big plantations were broken up into small farms operated by private landowners and sharecroppers. Individual farmers began to clear land in the late 1900s, and many small farms were established.

During the 1920s and 1930s, mechanized agriculture was introduced to the Delta. Small farmers could no longer make a living, so many moved to other states. From the 1950s to 1990s, large agricultural businesses established agribusinesses growing cotton, soybeans, sugar beets, and rice. Today, in addition to agriculture, the Delta region focuses on tourism related to its rich cultural history, including blues music and musicians. Delta cities have also focused on bringing automobile parts manufacturers, pharmaceutical companies, and other new industries to the area.

are the white-tailed deer and the red fox. States usually choose animals that are well known in the state to be official state animals. The Mississippi state bird is the mockingbird, and state reptile is the alligator. Mississippi also has a state water mammal: the bottle-nosed dolphin. With many freshwater lakes and streams, fishing is a popular sport and a way to catch food. As a result, the state fish is the largemouth bass, a well-known and popular game fish.

The Pearl River is one of Mississippi's major rivers. Its backwater is a swampy area reminiscent of the bayou in Louisiana or the Everglades in Florida.

According to the U.S. Department of Agriculture, more than twelve thousand plants grow in Mississippi. The state's best-known tree is the pecan tree, which is native to the Mississippi River floodplain. The pecan tree produces flavorful nuts that were a popular food for native peoples for thousands of years and continue to be popular today in cookies, pies, candy, and other dishes. The black-eyed Susan is a bright yellow flower that is native to Mississippi. Other plants include the pitcher plant, a carnivorous plant that holds water mixed with plant enzymes. Small insects are attracted to the liquid but become trapped and drown. The pitcher plant's enzymes then digest the insects, providing the plant with food.

Chapter 2

THE HISTORY OF MISSISSIPPI

Mississippi is named for the Mississippi River, which is the western boundary of the state and empties into the Gulf of Mexico. Based on Native American languages, at least two different native peoples have influenced the state name. The Chippewa words *mici zibi* mean "great river" or "gathering in of all the waters." The Algonquins used the word *Messipi* to refer to great waters.

With its rich, fertile land, Mississippi was home to native peoples for thousands of years. Native people first came to the area about twelve thousand years ago. One of the most fascinating early cultures is the Hopewell culture, also called the Mound Builders. Mounds are rectangular, flat-topped earth structures where native peoples erected temples or ceremonial centers. From about 2000 BCE to 1500 CE, mounds were built throughout Mississippi. Mississippi native peoples today include the Choctaw, which remain the only federally recognized American Indian tribe in Mississippi.

Years of Spanish and French Exploration

Today's Mississippi locales of De Soto County and the town of Hernando reflect the explorations of Spaniard Hernando de Soto. In the winter of 1540, de Soto led a group of about seven hundred Spanish explorers into Mississippi. De Soto was in search of gold or silver. By the spring of 1541, the group reached the Mississippi River.

One year later, having found no gold or silver, de Soto returned to the banks of the Mississippi, where he became ill and died. By this time, only three hundred men remained from the original expedition. Building seven boats, the remaining explorers journeyed down the Mississippi River and into the Gulf of Mexico, eventually reaching safety at a Spanish settlement in Mexico in December 1542.

A century and a half later, a small group of French Canadians explored the Mississippi River

This sixteenth-century portrait of Spanish explorer Hernando de Soto shows the hair and beard style common for Spanish gentlemen of his era. The armor shown in the picture is probably more elaborate than the ordinary armor worn by de Soto.

and saw how valuable control of the enormous river would be to France. René-Robert Cavelier, Sieur de La Salle, an ambitious explorer and fur trader, claimed Mississippi in 1682 as a French colony. French settlements were soon established along the river, including today's cities of New Orleans, Louisiana, and Biloxi, Mississippi.

As European explorers and colonists from different nations increased in number, conflicts began to break out. The French and Indian War was a seven-year war between England and the American colonies against the French and some of the Indians in North America. When the war ended in 1763, France was no longer in control of

American pioneer and frontiersman Jim Bowie gave his name to one of history's best-known hunting and combat knives. In 1827, his fight against several opponents on the sandbar near Natchez, Mississippi, was won by the use of his Bowie knife.

many of its previous territories, including large areas of Canada and the lower Mississippi Valley.

The oldest city on the Mississippi River is Natchez, which was founded in 1716 as the French Fort Rosalie. After the American Revolution (1775–1783), Spain regained possession of Florida and nearby regions and occupied Natchez, which remained under Spanish rule until 1798. The town of Vidalia is named for an early Spanish settler, Don Jose Vidal. In 1798, the area that was known as the Mississippi Territory joined the United States, becoming an official U.S. territory.

Territory to Statehood: 1798–1860

The original Mississippi Territory was organized in 1798 from land that had been disputed by the United States and Spain. The Mississippi Territory was expanded in 1804 and again in 1812 to extend from the Gulf of Mexico to the border of today's state of Tennessee. On March 3, 1817, Congress divided the Mississippi Territory. The western portion became the state of Mississippi, and the eastern became the Alabama Territory. Mississippi officially became the twentieth state on December 10, 1817.

During the years between statehood and the Civil War, the rapid growth of plantations and the opening of land in northern Mississippi at first had a wild frontier quality. The namesake of the Bowie knife, Jim Bowie, in 1827, fought a legendary duel against several men on a sandbar near Natchez, Mississippi. During the battle, Bowie was shot in the lung, stabbed, and beaten, but he still managed to win the fight by using his large Bowie knife.

Mississippi's economy was also growing rapidly. Between the time of its gaining statehood in 1817 to 1860, Mississippi became the most dynamic and largest cotton-producing state in America. The rapid rise of cotton production and worldwide demand led to a wealthy new culture of plantation owners in Mississippi in the 1830s.

Much of the Mississippi economy relied upon the slave labor, especially on the large cotton plantations. By 1840, slaves outnumbered free people, comprising 52 percent of Mississippi's population. The crop that they harvested, cotton, was so valuable that it was referred to as white gold.

Civil War Years and Confederacy: 1860–1864

In 1860, Abraham Lincoln was elected president of the United States. He was a member of the Republican Party, which opposed the expansion of slavery. At the time, Lincoln's policies seemed threatening to the ordinary way of life in Mississippi, even though the majority of Mississippians did not own slaves. Mississippi voted to secede, or leave, the United States on January 9, 1861.

After an initial period of enthusiasm, Mississippi began to experience the harsh realities of war. Food, materials, and labor shortages caused much suffering. Many Civil War battles were fought in

How the Civil Rights Movement Changed Mississippi

Today, historians look back on the conflicts and challenges of the civil rights era in the 1950s and 1960s and realize that change was inevitable. At the time, the civil rights movement inspired violence, fear, and intimidation. In 1962, rioting erupted over the admission of James Meredith, a black student, to the University of Mississippi. Another tragic incident occurred in 1964 when twenty-one-year-old James Chaney, a black Mississippian, and two white men from New York, Andrew Goodman, twenty, and Michael Schwerner, twenty-four, were brutally murdered by members of the Ku Klux Klan in Nashoba County, Mississippi. The three young men had been registering African Americans to vote when they were kidnapped and killed.

As the civil rights movement developed in the 1950s and 1960s, African American citizens demonstrated using techniques of nonviolent resistance pioneered by Mohandas Gandhi, a famous Indian leader. The ideas of Gandhi and other early advocates for human rights inspired Martin Luther King Jr. and other pioneers of the civil rights movement.

By the end of the 1960s, the civil rights movement had a positive effect. By 1970, nearly all formerly white colleges and universities in Mississippi were actively enrolling black students. Mississippi's elementary and high schools were desegregated, or made equally available to both African American and white students. By 1975, there were more African Americans in Mississippi state government than in any other state. By 2000, racial divisions were no longer the main issue in Mississippi. Social and economic development for all Mississippians was at last a reality in the twenty-first century.

Mississippi. More than seventy-eight thousand men left their homes in Mississippi to fight in the Civil War. Only twenty-seven thousand returned, and many of these men were injured and disabled.

Black Mississippians also fought. More than 17,000 joined the Union army to fight for freedom from slavery. After the end of the Civil War in 1865, 436,000 slaves in Mississippi became freedmen.

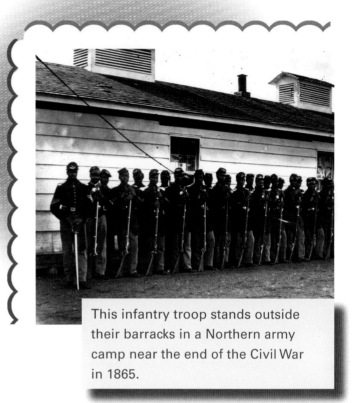

This infantry troop stands outside their barracks in a Northern army camp near the end of the Civil War in 1865.

Post–Civil War and Reconstruction: 1865–1900

Although they were no longer slaves, Mississippi's freedmen did not have land, and they had few opportunities for work. Enthusiastic about their freedom, former slaves helped the newly formed Mississippi Republican Party. They voted, helped to shape and implement constitutional reform, and served in offices at all government levels. Two former slaves, Hiram R. Revels and Blanche K. Bruce, were elected as U.S. senators during this time. In 1873, after serving as the first African American speaker of the Mississippi House of Representatives, John R. Lynch became the first African American to be elected to the U.S. House of Representatives. More than one

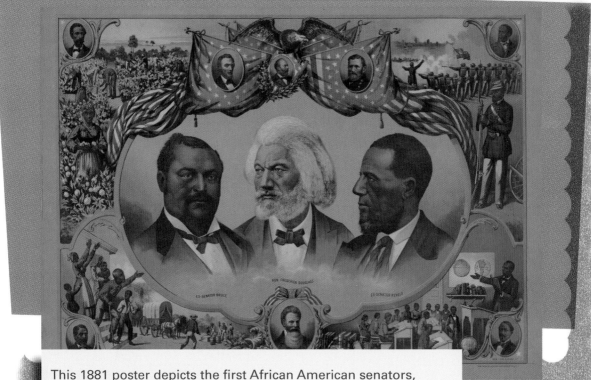

This 1881 poster depicts the first African American senators, Hiram Revels (*left*) and Blanche Kelso Bruce (*right*), with Frederick Douglass (*middle*), the former slave who used his writings to educate Americans about slavery.

hundred years later, in 1986, Mike Espy became the second African American from Mississippi to be elected to the U.S. House of Representatives.

All Mississippians were not ready to support African American voting rights and participation in government. The Reconstruction period after the Civil War was marred by groups of whites who terrorized African Americans to prevent them from voting or running for public office. In some areas, fewer than 5 percent of African Americans were registered to vote. So-called Jim Crow laws, which were meant to stop African Americans from voting, were passed during this time, preventing African Americans in Mississippi from voting and exercising their civil rights as citizens.

Twentieth-Century Struggles

Racial oppression and economic hardship combined to make the first half of the twentieth century a difficult one for Mississippi; it became America's poorest state. Federal programs during the Great Depression provided some help, but farmers, black and white, struggled to survive, after increasing mechanization resulted in less need for farm workers. Many farmers migrated to northern industrial states like Michigan and Illinois, or moved to larger cities in the south, like Memphis, Tennessee, and New Orleans, Louisiana.

World War II (1940–1944) put 23,700 Mississippians into military uniforms. Their service exposed them to a world that was very different from Mississippi. Veterans' benefits provided them with opportunities for college and better housing. Veterans both black and white were influenced by the goals of World War II to end racism and violence. However, some Mississippians continued to resist offering full civil rights and education to African Americans. Mississippi became known nationally as the southern state most resistant to civil equality for all races.

In the 1950s, a landmark U.S. Supreme Court decision, *Brown v. Board of Education*, declared that schools should be equal for all students, regardless of their race. Traditionally, Mississippi's schools had been separated, or segregated, between African American and white students. Segregated schools became one of the most powerful symbols of inequality for the civil rights movement that emerged throughout the south in the 1950s.

Chapter 3

THE GOVERNMENT OF MISSISSIPPI

Mississippi became a part of the United States as the Mississippi Territory in 1797. After the U.S. Congress divided the Mississippi Territory in half, with the eastern half becoming the Alabama Territory, the western half became the twentieth U.S. state in 1817. The first Mississippi Constitution was adopted in 1817, with amendments added in 1832 and 1869. The current state government operates under the Constitution of 1890. The state's laws are set forth in the Mississippi Code of 1972.

Constitutional amendments may be proposed by a two-thirds majority of the Mississippi legislature, which is a bicameral legislature, meaning that it includes both the state senate and the house of representatives. To become effective, an amendment must be approved by a majority of Mississippi citizens voting on the issue in a general election.

Executive Branch

The chief executive of Mississippi is the governor, who is elected to a four-year term and may not serve two successive terms. In case of death, removal from office, or incapacity to serve, the governor is

The 2008 presidential primary elections in Mississippi brought out many different voters who were inspired by the candidacy of President Barack Obama, America's first African American president.

succeeded by the lieutenant governor, who is also elected to a four-year term. Other elected executive officials include the secretary of state, the treasurer, the auditor of public accounts, the attorney general, the commissioner of agriculture and commerce, and the commissioner of insurance. Among the elected officials, the state treasurer is responsible for administering the state's budget and acting as a "watchdog for taxpayers," according to Tate Reeves, Mississippi state treasurer in 2009. Mississippi's state auditor also reviews government expenditures and prepares accounting reports to ensure that tax funds are spent appropriately.

Legislature

The Mississippi legislature consists of a 52-member state senate and a 122-member house of representatives. All legislators are elected to four-year terms. The Mississippi State Senate has more than forty committees that review state governance and prepare legislation, and the house of representatives has fifty committees.

The chief justice of the Mississippi Supreme Court is Bill Waller Jr. Justice Waller is a graduate of Mississippi State University and the son of the fifty-fifth governor of the state, Bill Waller Sr.

Judiciary

Mississippi's highest court is the state supreme court. Nine justices that are elected to eight-year terms serve on the court. Other courts are the chancery and circuit courts, with a total of seventy-nine judges popularly elected to four-year terms. Mississippi's chancery courts hear civil cases, or disputes involving money and property. Mississippi's circuit courts try both civil and criminal cases. Mississippi also has county, municipal, justice, and family courts.

Mississippi's elected attorney general administers the state's justice department, which operates divisions to protect consumers, oversee businesses and corporations, and help senior citizens, parents, and children, as well as specialized cybercrime and school safety divisions.

Local Government

Mississippi is divided into eighty-one counties, each of which is administered by an elected five-member board of supervisors. The state also has more than 290 incorporated cities and towns. Twenty of Mississippi's counties have names derived from the state's historical Native American residents, including Tunica, Chickasaw, and Choctaw counties.

National Representation

Mississippi elects four representatives to the U.S. House of Representatives and two senators to the U.S. Senate. The state has six electoral votes in the electoral college for presidential elections, a number that decreased from seven between the presidential elections of 2000 and 2004. This was because of a decrease in the state's population in the 2000 U.S. Census.

How a Bill Becomes a Law

Laws passed by the Mississippi legislature become laws using a similar process to most other U.S. states. First, bills are introduced by a senator or representative in the Mississippi house or senate. The bills are then referred to a committee, which conducts hearings and issues a report. If the bill receives a positive recommendation

The Life of Fannie Lou Hamer and Voting Rights

One of the best ways to understand the change in government and voting in Mississippi is through the life of one of the civil rights movement's heroes, Fannie Lou Hamer. Fannie Hamer was born in 1917, the youngest of twenty children in her African American family. She was the granddaughter of a slave, and her parents, Jim and Ella Thompson, were sharecroppers. Hamer began picking cotton at age six and was forced to drop out of school in sixth grade to help support her family. After marrying a sharecropper, Hamer continued to farm until 1962, when she decided that she wanted to vote. At the time, it was extremely difficult for African Americans to vote in Mississippi.

On August 31, 1962, Hamer took a bus with seventeen others to Indianola, Mississippi, where she registered to vote. On the way home, police stopped the bus and arrested Hamer and the others. Hamer, her husband, and others trying to vote were forced to leave the plantation where they farmed and were later shot at, threatened, imprisoned, and beaten.

During the 1964 U.S. presidential elections, a new party called the Mississippi Freedom Democratic Party (MFDP) sent a delegation, including Hamer, to the national Democratic Party Convention. Hamer spoke to the convention about voting injustices. A year later, President Lyndon Baines Johnson signed the Voting Rights Act. By the time Hamer died in 1977, all citizens of Mississippi were not only entitled to vote—they did vote, without fear or interference.

Fannie Lou Hamer was able to educate and advocate using her quick wit and way with words.

and vote from the committee that reviews it and reports on it, the bill is placed on the senate or house calendar for debate and a vote.

If, after debate, the bill is passed by a majority of members of the house or senate, it is then referred to the other branch of the legislature, which follows a similar process. After passage by the other branch, the bill may undergo changes. A conference committee with members from both the house and senate is appointed to review the two bills and consolidate them, compromising when necessary. A conference report is issued, and the new joint bill is then returned to both the house and senate for another vote.

Following a successful vote and passage of the bill by both the house and senate, the bill has made it through the entire legislative process. Then it is sent to the executive branch, the office of the Mississippi governor. The governor may sign the bill into law or may veto the bill. A veto means that the governor refuses to sign the bill and sends it back to the legislature. The bill will only become law if the legislature overturns the veto by a two-thirds vote. Another option is for the governor to refuse to sign the bill by the annual deadline set by the legislature, which means that the bill becomes law but the governor has not given it his or her official approval by signing it.

Chapter 4

THE ECONOMY OF MISSISSIPPI

Mississippi's economy has always been rooted in its land, the Mississippi River, and its warm, humid climate. Native peoples in Mississippi historically farmed, fished, and lived off the land in a sustainable way. The Natchez Indians who lived in southwestern Mississippi were successful farmers, growing corn, beans, and squash. They also hunted, fished, and gathered wild plants.

During the sixteenth century, Spanish explorer Hernando de Soto explored the region around the Mississippi River searching for gold and silver. No precious metals were found by the explorer. Instead, the rich Mississippi land created opportunities for agriculture, which eventually became dominated by cotton. For most of the state's history, cotton was the backbone of Mississippi's traditional agricultural economy, and at one point before the Civil War, cotton brought great wealth to some residents. Cotton production suffered extreme declines after the Civil War, in the 1860s, and during the Great Depression in the 1930s.

After many years of a slow economy that contributed to the poverty of the state's residents, Mississippi's economy today is thriving, with diversified and sustainable agriculture and new industries. Although Mississippi's economic structure is changing, it is

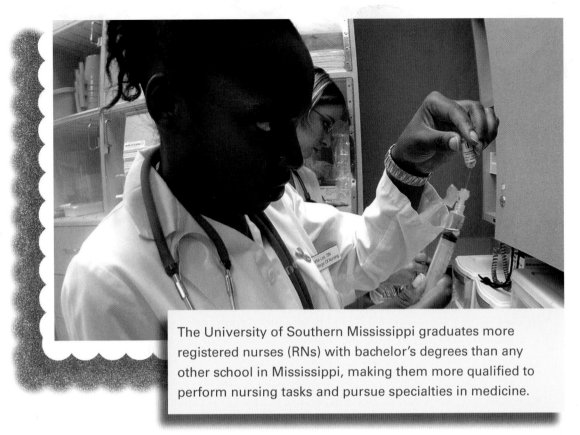

The University of Southern Mississippi graduates more registered nurses (RNs) with bachelor's degrees than any other school in Mississippi, making them more qualified to perform nursing tasks and pursue specialties in medicine.

different from the economy found in most other states. Compared to other states, Mississippi has large government, manufacturing, transportation, trade, and utilities sectors. Together, these sectors accounted for 53.3 percent of Mississippi's total nonagricultural employment in November 2008, compared to 44.8 percent for the United States as a whole.

Economic sectors that are smaller in Mississippi than other states include education, health care, financial services, and professional business services. These sectors combined accounted for 32.9 percent of employment in the United States overall in 2008, but only 23.8 percent in Mississippi.

PAST AND PRESENT

Mississippi's Agriculture

Mississippi's agricultural past was dominated by cotton plantations, which were operated first by African American slaves and then by sharecroppers. Sharecropping is a form of farming where individual farmers receive plots of land to farm in exchange for giving a share of their crops to the landowners.

The most fertile cotton-growing area of Mississippi was the Mississippi Delta, located in the northwestern part of the state. In this area, floods were common until levees were built after the Civil War. A levee is an earth structure similar to a dam that protects outlying areas from flooding. After the Civil War, a new group of landowners drained the fertile land in the Delta, cleared the forests, and began to plant large amounts of cotton. Although these large post–Civil War farms did not use any type of slave labor, they were still usually referred to as plantations.

Today, the Mississippi Delta is still home to many large plantations. However, the agricultural products that are produced are no longer processed by hand. Mississippi's current farm industry is highly mechanized. Agriculture remains one of the top sources of jobs in Mississippi, employing about 29 percent of the state's work force. However, cotton is no longer the dominant crop that it was for much of the state's history. The top five agricultural products in 2009 were poultry and eggs, lumber, soybeans, corn, and catfish. Cotton is the eighth agricultural product on Mississippi's agricultural list according to the Mississippi Department of Agriculture and Commerce.

This 1883 painting is called *The Sunny South*. Mississippi still has a strong agricultural economy, but the picture represents the plantation farming of the past.

Manufacturing

About 250,000 people in Mississippi are employed in manufacturing, which accounts for about 28 percent of the annual gross state product. The annual earnings of the manufacturing industry exceed $10 billion. Pascagoula is the state's main industrial center. Among Mississippi's leading manufactured products are transportation equipment; clothing and textiles;

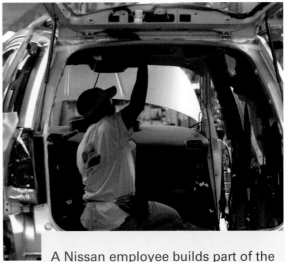

A Nissan employee builds part of the interior of a minivan at the Nissan assembly plant in Canton, Mississippi.

lumber, furniture, and other wood products; electronic goods; and processed foods. Aerospace equipment and motor-vehicle parts are also manufactured. Wood products, including household furniture, are manufactured in many cities, including Tupelo, Columbus, Jackson, and Natchez. Corinth and Jackson are the chief centers for producing electronic equipment. Major industries that have established plants in Mississippi include Toyota, Nissan, and Viking.

Farming and Food Production

In addition to agricultural products like poultry, eggs, soybeans, and corn, aquaculture is an important industry in Mississippi. Fishing and commercial fish farming provide significant economic growth for Mississippi. Between the Mississippi River and the Gulf Coast,

This park commemorates Natchez, Mississippi, the oldest established settlement on the Mississippi River. Though first settled by French explorers, Spanish and American frontier culture also helped create this beautiful city.

Mississippi is among the top shrimp-producing states in America. The state leads the nation in commercially raised catfish production.

Tourism and Entertainment

Although it is only the sixth-largest category in Mississippi's overall economy, tourism and entertainment accounted for eighty-five thousand jobs in Mississippi in 2008. These jobs represent about 8 percent of the jobs in Mississippi. Tourism also accounted for more than thirty thousand indirectly created jobs in 2008. Mississippi is one of the leading states in casino or gambling income; in 1992, Mississippi began to license casinos for operation. Since that time, jobs and income related to casinos have expanded the state economy, particularly in areas along the Mississippi River and the Gulf Coast. Mississippi's Gulf Coast, along with Louisiana's, was devastated by Hurricane Katrina in 2005. Tourism-related industry in the Gulf area, especially near Biloxi, was damaged and was slow to recover.

Other tourism in Mississippi is related to the state's rich cultural history, including the Blues Museum in Clarksdale, the Natchez historical area, and many Civil War–related points of interest.

Chapter 5

PEOPLE FROM MISSISSIPPI: PAST AND PRESENT

Mississippi is the birthplace or home of many famous musicians, authors, civil rights leaders, scientists, and entrepreneurs.

Historic Mississippians

René-Robert Cavelier, Sieur de La Salle (1643–1687)
René-Robert Cavelier, Sieur de La Salle, was the first European to navigate the Mississippi River all the way from its headwaters to the Gulf of Mexico. La Salle explored the Great Lakes in Canada and the United States, the Mississippi River, and the Gulf of Mexico. La Salle claimed territory in Mississippi and Louisiana for France, leading to French settlements at New Orleans and Natchez, Mississippi.

Hernando de Soto (c. 1496/97–1542) In 1530, Spanish explorer Hernando de Soto first served as part of Francisco Pizarro's forces in the Spanish conquest of Peru. Later, de Soto became governor of the island of Cuba and was asked to explore and colonize the North American continent. He was probably the first European to see the Mississippi River.

Scientists and Researchers

Arthur Guyton (1919–2003)
Dr. Arthur Guyton was born in Oxford, Mississippi. He practiced at the University of Mississippi Medical Center and is regarded as the top cardiovascular physician of the twentieth century. Guyton suffered from polio—a disease that causes paralysis—which today has been nearly eliminated through vaccination. As part of his recovery from polio, he invented the first motorized wheelchair, receiving a presidential citation among many other honors.

Rene-Robert Cavelier, Sieur de la Salle, was the first French explorer to lead groups of French-Canadian settlers down the Mississippi River. French settlements included today's cities of New Orleans, Louisiana, and Biloxi, Mississippi.

James D. Hardy (1918–2003) Dr. James D. Hardy, who grew up in Alabama, was chairman of the Department of Surgery at the University of Mississippi in Jackson from 1955 until 1987. In 1963 and 1964, Hardy performed the first human lung and heart transplants.

Elizabeth Lee Hazen (1885–1975) Elizabeth Lee Hazen was born in Rich, Mississippi. In 1905, she became one of the first female chemists, graduating with a Ph.D. from

Oprah Winfrey

One of the world's most powerful and popular media figures, Oprah Winfrey is known worldwide. Born January 29, 1954, on a farm in Kosciusko, Mississippi, Oprah's life story is inspirational to millions worldwide. Oprah began "performing" at only age three, while she was being raised by her grandmother. Later, she experienced poverty and abuse, and she was almost sent to a juvenile detention facility at age thirteen. Sent to live with her father, Vernon Winfrey, Oprah obeyed his curfew and read a book every week, writing up a report for her father. By age seventeen, Oprah had her first radio show in Nashville, and two years later, she had her first television show.

After graduating from Tennessee State University, Oprah moved to Baltimore, and later to Chicago, where she established her broadcasting career and currently bases her international media empire, HARPO Entertainment Group.

Oprah's work to prevent child abuse resulted in the passage of the National Child Protection Act, also called Oprah's Bill, in 1993. Oprah has been named as one of the one hundred most influential people of the twentieth century by *Time* magazine, and she received a lifetime achievement award from the National Academy of Television Arts and Sciences in 1998. She received the National Book Club's Fiftieth Anniversary Gold Award in 1998 for her promotion of reading and books through her famous book club, which has launched the careers of many authors and promoted the reading and sales of millions of books.

In 2003, *Forbes* magazine reported that Oprah was the first African American woman to become a billionaire. No other person from Mississippi better illustrates the positive change that has occurred in the state from the days of poverty and slavery to the present.

Columbia University. She created the world's first effective antifungal antibiotic, called nystatin.

Civil Rights Leaders

Medgar Evers (1925–1963) Civil rights leader Medgar Wiley Evers was born in Decatur, Mississippi. After serving in the U.S. Army during World War II, Evers returned to Mississippi and completed his education at Alcorn State University, where he excelled as a student. After graduation, he married Myrlie Beasley (now

The life of Medgar Evers, one of the civil rights movement's most famous and revered leaders, was cut short in 1963, when he was assassinated by an opponent of equal rights.

known as Myrlie Evers-Williams), also a pioneering civil rights leader. Evers worked to eliminate segregation in public places. He championed the admission of black student James Meredith to "Ole Miss," the University of Mississippi, which had previously been an all-white school. Rioting and violence surrounded James's admission to the university. Medgar Evers was murdered on June 12, 1963.

Authors and Playwrights

William Faulkner, Nobel Prize–winning author and Mississippi native, invented an entire community called Yoknapatawpha County, inspired by folklore representing the rich culture and history of Mississippi.

William Faulkner (1897–1962) William Faulkner, one of America's most famous and influential authors, was in New Albany, Mississippi. The only person from Mississippi to ever win a Nobel Prize, Faulkner's novels were once out of print before he received international recognition for his writing, winning the Nobel Prize 1949.

Jim Henson (1936–1990) Born in Greenville, Mississippi, Jim Henson was one of the world's most famous puppeteers. He created many of the Muppets' most memorable characters including Kermit the Frog, Miss Piggy, and Elmo. Many of these characters appeared on shows such as *Sesame Street* and the *Muppet Show* as well as in the film *The Muppet Movie*.

Tennessee Williams (1911–1983) Tennessee Williams, a Pulitzer Prize–winning playwright, whose plays include *A*

Streetcar Named Desire, *The Glass Menagerie*, and *Cat on a Hot Tin Roof*, was born in Columbus, Mississippi. Williams's plays were often based upon his own family and upbringing in Mississippi.

Famous Entertainers and Entrepreneurs

Robert Johnson (1911–1938) Robert Johnson, who is called the Grandfather of Rock and Roll, was born in Hazlehurst, Mississippi. He died in 1938 in Greenville, Mississippi, but his famous musical styles have influenced hundreds of musicians since that time.

Riley "B. B." King (1925–) Pioneer of the electric blues guitar, Riley "B. B." King was born in Itta Bena, Mississippi. Still recording and performing music in 2009, B. B. King is one of the most recognized blues musicians in the world.

Robert Pittman (1953–) Music television pioneer Robert Pittman was born in Jackson, Mississippi. In 1981, he created the programming for MTV, the world's most famous and successful cable music television network.

Elvis Presley (1935–1977) Elvis Presley, one of the world's best-known musicians, was born in Tupelo, Mississippi. The two-bedroom house where Elvis was born was built by his father for a cost of only $180. Today, the house and a surrounding fifteen-acre park are top tourist attractions in Tupelo.

Timeline

1541	Spanish explorer Hernando de Soto first sees the Mississippi River at a site near today's town of Clarksdale, Mississippi.
1817	Mississippi becomes the twentieth U.S. state.
1841	Blanche K. Bruce, the first African American to serve a full term in the U.S. Senate, is born.
1861	Mississippi becomes the second Southern state to secede from the Union.
1894	Joseph A. Biedenham, a pharmacist in Vicksburg, Mississippi, is the first person to bottle Coca-Cola.
1900	John Luther "Casey" Jones, a train engineer, wrecks his train near Vaughn, Mississippi, but heroically saves the passengers, inspiring a famous song, "The Legend of Casey Jones."
1911	Blues musician Robert Johnson is born in Hazlehurst. He later becomes known as the Grandfather of Rock and Roll and the Father of the Blues.
1925	B. B. King, the King of the Blues, is born in Itta Bena, Mississippi.
1927	The Mississippi River breaks the levee at Mounds Landing, near Scott, Mississippi, causing the Great Flood of 1927.
1962	Fanny Lou Hamer attempts unsuccessfully to register to vote in the Sunflower County Courthouse in Indianola, Mississippi, and begins her campaign for voting rights.
1963	Dr. James D. Hardy becomes the first physician to perform a human lung transplant at the University of Mississippi Medical Center.
1964	Mississippi's "Freedom Summer" becomes a landmark time for the civil rights movement.
1986	Mike Espy becomes the first African American to be elected to the U.S. Congress since Reconstruction.
2005	Hurricane Katrina devastates the Gulf Coast of Mississippi and Louisiana.
2009	James A. Young is elected the first African American mayor of Philadelphia, Mississippi, the town where three civil rights workers were killed by the Ku Klux Klan in 1964.

Mississippi at a Glance

State motto:	*Virtue et armis*, a Latin phrase meaning "by valor and arms"
State capital:	Jackson
State tree:	Magnolia
State bird:	Mockingbird
State flower:	Magnolia
Year of statehood:	December 10, 1817; the twentieth state
State nickname:	The Magnolia State
Total area and U.S. rank:	48,434 square miles (125,443 sq km; thirty-second)
Population:	2,939,000
Length of coastline:	44 miles (71 km)
Highest elevation:	806 feet (245.66 m), Woodall Mountain
Lowest elevation:	Sea level, at the Gulf of Mexico

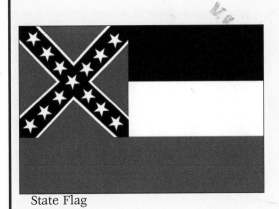

State Flag

State Seal

Major rivers:	Mississippi River, Yazoo River, Pascagoula River
Major lakes:	Sardis Lake, Arkabutla Lake, Grenada Lake
Hottest recorded temperature:	115°F (46°C) in 1930 in Holly Springs
Coldest recorded temperature:	-18 °F (-27.7°C) in 1966 in Corinth
Origin of state name:	Taken from the Mississippi River, the name of which is derived from a Native American term for "big river."
Chief agricultural products:	Eggs and poultry, timber, corn, soybeans, and catfish
Major industries:	Agriculture and manufacturing

Mockingbird

Magnolia

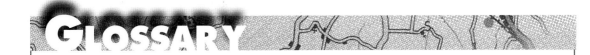

alluvial plain A wide, flat landform created over a long period of time by sediments or soil deposited by one or more rivers.

civil rights movement A historical period during the 1950s and 1960s when African Americans and others sought equal rights as citizens, including voting rights, economic rights, and education.

Civil War Also called the War Between the States, the Civil War was fought from 1861 to 1865 between eleven Southern states, which all supported slavery, and the Northern states, which did not support slavery.

delta A delta is a wide, fertile plain caused by the flooding of large rivers. In Mississippi, the Delta is formed by the flood plain of the Yazoo and Mississippi rivers.

Jim Crow laws A group of laws passed in southern states between 1876 and 1965 meant to provide "separate but equal" facilities, services, and programs for African American and white residents. Jim Crow laws were finally eliminated after the civil rights movement of the 1950s and 1960s.

levee An earth structure similar to a dam that protects farms and towns from river flooding. The Mississippi River is so large that levees are necessary in all of its bordering states, including Mississippi.

plantation The traditional name for a large farm owned by a wealthy grower and operated by slaves. Plantations remain today, but they are operated by small farmers who own their land and grow their own crops.

racism A belief that people's human rights, intelligence, or talents are based upon race and that one race is superior to others, leading to discrimination and segregation.

Reconstruction The historical period following the U.S. Civil War (1861–1865), when African Americans began to gain voting rights and were elected to government offices, only to be later excluded by Jim Crow laws.

segregation A social and political process meant to keep separate facilities between different races, including schools, stores, sports teams, public transportation, and public facilities, including restrooms.

slavery An economic system where some people lack human rights and opportunity and are forced to work for others and are regarded as their property.

Center for the Study of Southern Culture

The University of Mississippi

P.O. Box 1848

University, MS 38677

(662) 915-5993

Web site: http://www.olemiss.edu/depts/south/index.html

Dedicated to researching, documenting, and providing information about the culture of the American South, the center produces television and radio programming, conferences, and exhibits and offers many resources for students and members of the public.

Delta Blues Museum

1 Blues Alley Lane

Clarksdale, MS 38614

(662) 627-6820

Web site: http://www.deltabluesmuseum.org

The Delta Blues Museum features instruments, photos of musicians, memorabilia, and interactive exhibits about blues music and the cultural history of the Mississippi Delta.

Mississippi Cares

P.O. Box 9745

Mississippi State, MS 39762-9745

(662) 325-3080

Web site: http://msucares.com

Part of the Federal Cooperative Extension system, the Mississippi State University Extension Service provides information and conducts research on agriculture, the environment, nutrition, and many other important topics, including sponsoring Mississippi 4-H programs for youth.

Mississippi Council on Economic Education

Mississippi State University

326 McCool Hall

Box 9580

Mississippi State, MS 39762

(662) 325-1987

Web site: http://misweb.cbi.msstate.edu

The council provides outreach, programs, and education on personal finance, sound finan-cial habits, and financial literacy for Mississippi teachers and students in grades K–12.

Mississippi Department of Marine Resources

1141 Bayview Avenue

Biloxi, MS 39530

(800) 374-3449

Web site: http://www.dmr.state.ms.us

The department provides online and in-person resources for the public on fishing, water quality, wetlands, and many more aspects of Mississippi's Gulf Coast.

The William Faulkner Society

Department of English

The University of Mississippi

University, MS 38677-1848

Web site: http://www.olemiss.edu

The William Faulkner Society provides student scholarships, sponsors an annual Yonknapatawpha conference named after the fictional county based on Oxford, Mississippi, featured in Faulkner's stories, and publishes a newsletter and other resources on Mississippi's most famous author.

Web Sites

Due to the changing nature of Internet links, Rosen Publishing has developed an online list of Web sites related to the subject of this book. This site is updated regularly. Please use this link to access the list:

http://www.rosenlinks.com/uspp/mspp

Bowers, Rick. *Spies of the Mississippi*. Washington, DC: National Geographic Children's Books, 2010.

Crowe, Chris. *Mississippi Trial: 1955*. New York, NY: Speak, 2003.

Currie, Stephen. *Crime Scene Investigations: Murder in Mississippi—the 1964 Freedom Summer Killings*. Farmington Hills, MI: Lucent, 2006.

Deutsch, Stacia, and Rhody Cohon. *Hot Pursuit: Murder In Mississippi*. Minneapolis, MI: Kar-Ben Books, 2010.

Gaines, Ann. *Mississippi* (It's My State!). Salt Lake City, UT: Benchmark Books, 2007.

Johnson, Robin. *The Mississippi: America's Mighty River*. New York, NY: Crabtree, 2006.

Marsh, Carol. *Native American Heritage: Mississippi Indians*. Peachtree City, GA: Gallopade, 2004.

Miller, Mary Carol. *Must See Mississippi: 50 Favorite Places*. Jackson, MS: University Press of Mississippi, 2007.

Tucker, Judy, ed. *Growing Up in Mississippi*. Jackson, MS: University Press of Mississippi, 2008.

Vander Zee, Ruth. *Mississippi Morning*. Grand Rapids, MI: Eerdmans Books, 2004.

BIBLIOGRAPHY

AAA Native Arts. "Mississippi Tribes." Retrieved August 11, 2009 (http://www.aaan ativearts.com/tribes-by-states/mississippi_tribes.htm).

ABC News. "The Big Six: Other Civil Rights Leaders." August 23, 2003. Retrieved September 25, 2009 (http://abcnews.go.com/WNT/story?id=129484).

The American Academy of Achievement. "Oprah Winfrey Biography." March 10, 2009. Retrieved September 21, 2009 (http://www.achievement.org/autodoc/page/win0bio-1).

Anderson, Peter C., and T. E. Crocker. "The Pecan Tree." University of Florida IAFS Extension. Retrieved September, 22, 2009 (http://edis.ifas.ufl.edu/HS229).

Bolton, Charles. "School Desegregation in Mississippi." Civil Rights Timeline. ...rsit... of Southern Mississippi, June 17, 2003. Retrieved September 25, 2009 (h... usm.edu/crdp/html/cd/desegregation.htm).

Carson, Thomas, and Mary Bonk, eds. "Mississippi." *Gale Encyclopedia of U...* *History*. Vol. 2. Detroit, MI: Gale, 2000.

Drapala, Patti. "Survey Reveals Growing Niche for Native Plants." *Mississ...* ...s, Vol. 5, No. 3, Summer, 2009, pp. 12–14.

Gunther, William. "The Mississippi Economic Outlook." *Entrepreneur*. S... pp. 51–54. (http://www.entrepreneur.com/tradejournals/article/p... 179031791.html).

The Lady Bird Johnson Wildflower Center. "Mississippi Recommended University of Texas at Austin. Retrieved September 28, 2009 (http: flower.org/collections/collection.php?start=10&collection=MS...).

Mississippi Department of Agriculture and Commerce. "Mississippi Overview." Retrieved August 10, 2009 (http://www.mdac.state.i... misc/ag_overview.html).

Northeast Mississippi Community College. "Mississippi People." M... ... ...d September 20, 2009 (http://www2.nemcc.edu/mspeople/).

Palmer, Colin A., ed. "Life in Mississippi: An Interview with Fannie Lou Hamer (1965)." *Encyclopedia of African-American Culture and History*. Vol. 6., 2nd ed. Detroit, MI: Macmillan Reference USA, 2006.

University of Mississippi Medical Center. "The Guyton Biography." The Arthur Guyton Archives, September 1, 2009. Retrieved September 20, 2009 (http://www.umc.edu/about_us/guyton_biography.html).

University of Mississippi Medical Center. "A Pioneer in Surgery." The James D. Hardy
Archives, September 1, 2009. Retrieved September 20, 2009 (http://www.umc.edu/
about_us/hardy.html).

U.S. Department of Commerce. "State Personal Income 2007." Bureau of Economic
Analysis. Retrieved August 10, 2009 (http://www.bea.gov/newsreleases/regional/
spi/2008/spi0308.htm).

U.S. Department of the Interior. "Ancient Architects of the Mississippi."
National Parks Service Archaeology Program, September 13, 2007.
Retrieved October 1, 2009 (http://www.nps.gov/history/archeology/feature/
builder.htm).

About the Author

Amy Sterling Casil is an award-nominated writer. She has published twenty books, including several written for the Rosen Publishing Group. She has a master's degree in literature and creative writing from Chapman University in Orange, California, and has taught composition and literature in diverse Southern California classrooms for ten years. Since 2005, she has also served as the vice president for development with Beyond Shelter, a nationally recognized nonprofit organization. She has traveled to Mississippi and toured the Mississippi Delta cultural area.

Photo Credits

Cover (top left), p. 17 MPI/Hulton Archive/Getty Images; cover (top right), pp. 3, 7, 12, 20, 26, 32, 38 Scott Olson/Getty Images; cover (bottom), p. 40 (right) Shutterstock.com; p. 4 (top) © GeoAtlas, Inc; p. 8 US Army Corps of Engineers, Mississippi Valley Division; p. 9 Bloomberg via Getty Images; p. 11 Charlie Brenner; p. 13 SuperStock/Getty Images; p. 14 The Texas State Preservation Board, Austin, Texas; pp. 18, 24 Library of Congress Prints and Photographs Division; p. 21 Marianne Todd/Getty Images; p. 22 Russ Houston © Mississippi State University 2008; p. 27 University of Southern Mississippi Photo by Steve Rouse; p. 28 Buyenlarge/Hulton Archive/Getty Images; p. 29 KRT/Newscom; p. 30 VOA/Newscom; p. 33 Archive Photos/Getty Images; p. 35 Hulton Archive/Getty Images; p. 36 Eric Schaal/Time & Life Pictures/Getty Images; p. 39 (left) Courtesy of Robesus, Inc.; p. 40 (left) Gary Kramer/U.S. Fish & Wildlife Service

Designer: Les Kanturek; Editor: Nick Croce; Photo Researcher: Peter Tomlinson